FROM THE HEART
Unlocked & Unplugged
VOL. 1

by

Jon Graham

DORRANCE
PUBLISHING CO
EST. 1920
PITTSBURGH, PENNSYLVANIA 15238

The contents of this work, including, but not limited to, the accuracy of events, people, and places depicted; opinions expressed; permission to use previously published materials included; and any advice given or actions advocated are solely the responsibility of the author, who assumes all liability for said work and indemnifies the publisher against any claims stemming from publication of the work.

Dorrance Publishing Co
585 Alpha Drive
Pittsburgh, PA 15238
Visit our website at *www.dorrancebookstore.com*

ISBN: 978-1-6491-3386-1
eISBN: 978-1-6491-3523-0

FROM THE HEART

Unlocked & Unplugged

VOL. 1

ACKNOWLEDGEMENTS

 First of all, I want to thank God, my Lord and Savior for blessing me with a hidden love and talent for poetry that I never imagined I would develop. I want to thank my mother and father, Mrs. Karen Graham and Mr. Ernie Graham, for I am not who I am today without them. It's been an unbelievable stress reliever for me throughout the years and has given my heart and my mind a sense of freedom.

I want to say 'thank you' to all of my friends who have encouraged me to keep writing and eventually become more comfortable with sharing my poetry. Those who have known me a long time know that sharing was not the easiest thing for me to do.

This is a collection of poetry I've written starting in 2011 leading up to 2019. It contains love, mystery, heartbreak, learning what love feels like again after heartache, and my overall thoughts on things that myself and all of us may go through in life. This is the story of a young teenager finding a new way to express himself as he goes through the tricky, more awkward stages of life, and as his mind and heart evolve, so does his poetry. This has for sure been a long time coming, I am more than happy to present to you all my peace, and my second no-longer-hidden passion. Welcome to *Unlocked and Unplugged*. I hope you enjoy it.

2011

So Fresh

Inspired by CJ Hilton's "So Fresh"

I've never met someone like you,
Guess I'm the lucky one since I caught you,
And my world changed the day that I got next to you,
She made me seasick, had my face turning blue.

Feeling like forever, or at least I thought it was,
Had her in my arms, loved her just because,
The way that we were felt like such a buzz,
She's got me hooked, because that's what she does.

The headline of us together reads "unstoppable,"
Gotta have the best, or have the incredible;
It's subliminal, blazing, straight up beautiful,
One of the freshest around, not to easily be winnable.

Love the way she looks at me,
Bad as she wanna be,
Love the way you move,
The way you do it, oh so smooth.

Don't matter what I'm going through;
You'll be there to see me through,
And girl, you already know, this is how we do,
And you wonder why I call her my boo,
So fresh like the ocean blue.

Bright city lights shining like your eyes,
It always looks better with the night skies;

I sit and daydream while the plane flies.
I want the mental strength to help me rise.

You text me saying that you love me,
But let's be real, do you really want to love me forever?
J. Cole made me think about that,
Because nowadays I wonder, do we really know what love really is?

What passion is? What hurt really is?
What trust really is?
These are the questions you want to ask yourself and your significant other.

Waking up with a clogged mind and mixed emotions, tell me…
How can you solve that?

The Voices in My Head

The voices in my head are lying;
I hear the words "failure," and "loser," and "the dream is dying,"
But I'm here to say, this is something I'm not buying,
Though there have been so many nights when I feel like crying.

I've been through way too much to just quit,
I've seen too much, life taking too much of a hit.
The voices in my head are negative,
But I say forget the negative; I must be positive.

I'm my worst enemy, my greatest nemesis;
One side is right, and the other is wrong, major differences.
I knew going in that it wouldn't be easy,
But I didn't think it would be hard either, sleazy.

The voices in my head, I hear fall.
But me, myself, God and I, we say rise.
Rise to success, success to basketball,
Success in life, no matter what the challenge size.

I heard the voices in my head talking,
And I ignore it, I keep moving.
The voices in my heard say, "Jon Graham is done,"
But Jon Graham says, "Hell no, I'm just beginning to have some fun."

The answers I want are invisible,
Not to be seen or heard, non-recognizable;
The answers I need, may be, in a way, pointless to seek,
For only God knows them, but I can at least continue to compete.

One More Time

I wish I could love, you just one more time;
I wanna hold you in my arms just one more time;
I want you all to myself, just one more time.
I don't mind living in a part of my past one more time.

If it's for the last time, then it is what it is;
I may not enjoy it, but that's what it is.
Never should've left you; don't know what I was doing,
Wish I had one more time to fix what I was thinking.

If I had a one more time, I might not have left you,
You still could've been my number one fan, too;
In my head, on rainy days, or when the sky's blue,
Is it too late to ask for one more time with you?

I may never get you out of my head,
Even though in my mind I feel like you have,
Though I can't undo what's been said,
I wish one more time that it's you I can have.

Murder my heart, she wrote,
Give me back my girl, then you give me back my life, I quote.
Never been another, not even close, like this,
I feel like I'm in the middle of a twist.

We were an unstoppable duo,
But now we play for different teams.
If I had just one wish, I'd wish
For one more chance, one more time,
With the true women of my biggest dreams.

Jon Graham

You know who you are…

2012

Fantasy vs. Reality

To me, my fantasy vs. my reality feels like a mystery,
A maze, a paradox, uncharted territory;
The mystery of my fantasy is what I feel,
The story of my reality is what is believed to be real.

My fantasy is what I want, but actually couldn't have;
The reality is what was in front of me, but didn't know I needed.
My emotions and hormones may want fantasy,
But mind, my spirit, my heart needs reality.

Most of the time, fantasy is what won't happen,
And reality is what needs to happen;
Reality becomes the certain,
And fantasy takes the back seat.

But fantasy won't go away; it stays there,
But reality came first, can never be erased anywhere.
I want fantasy sometimes, a lot,
But I need reality that much more than just a lot.

Fantasy may ultimately lose;
In the end, reality more than likely wins.
My eyes may get glued to an image of fantasy,
Because sometimes reality has the image we may not want to see.

Reality is truth, and the truth hurts,
So does it mean reality hurts?
But the truth is also a gift, so does it make reality a gift?

My reality tells my future,
Fantasy is a part of my dreams;

It reveals my suppressed thoughts,
Reality eventually shows the relevance of those thoughts.

Reality is, fantasy can be fool's gold;
Reality is the truest of stories ever to be told.
I may not be hurt, but may cry secretly with fantasy;
I may hurt, but will find my happiness with reality.

Jon Graham

Untitled

Everything that you are to me,
Is everything a magical wish could be,
My heart burns with the flames of passion,
Passion for you, not just talk, but action.

My past can be a visible angel of darkness,
But you are a brighter ray of hope, justice,
Restoring the wounds of my broken trust,
My broken insight, my broken love, unjust.

I feel your soft skin with my hands,
And also with my skin as we kiss;
Must say, heaven never felt closer,
Feel the warmth, a warmth only you can bring.

I feel my heart singing your name;
It can't deny what it truly feels,
What it truly wants, what it truly needs.
My heart can sing love again.

This may not rhyme that much,
But this… this feels better than rhymes,
This is life, it feels right, it feels clutch;
Everything you are to me, silences the hurtful times.

In your eyes, I see pain,
But at the same time, I see that you want your savior;
I will be what you need for as long as you want,
But we are stronger together than we are apart.

It took me a long time,
But I realized that, what I needed,
All I wanted, and what made me truly shine,
And help me stand up and fight against my worst enemy within, was you.

My strength, my sunlight, my love,
My everything, my beautiful wish:
This is a statement from my heart,
And an ode from the small tear I shed while writing this, for you.

2013

A Battle from Within

I got trouble on my mind;
Keep my eyes open all night, and it ain't because of the grind,
And I ask, why is freedom so hard to find?
I felt it at its best in the days when I shined.

Now darkness has covered the horizon,
And the future still signals me, no Verizon.
Darkness is at its peak right before the dawn;
The dawn can take a while, but until then, got to respond.

Life isn't everything that I've wanted yet,
But I'm blessed for where it's taken me.
Yet, I still want a lot more,
Call me greedy if you want, but I'm hungry for more.

Hungry for freedom, and my independence,
The journey to my destiny, must be relentless,
The game ain't what it used to be; I like it that way,
Because I'm not what I used to be, but I look familiar.

But the stress is constantly,
Can't understand stress, and stress doesn't understand me.

Sweat gushing down my face,
Mixed with my blood and my tears, my mind in outer space,
Mind running forever at such a fast pace,
Almost like it skipped time, but I know that isn't the case.

I'm quick to go to anger, hatred, despair,
When life goes south with all I can't bear,

But life waits for no one; doesn't matter if it's not fair.
Tough time in my life, I keep going only because I care.

Dug my way out of the bottom,
Feels like I'm falling back in,
Couldn't even see the top,
Now it gets harder to see the light.

The darkness breathes, but it can't win,
Because I am the shield, trying to protect my faith, my heart, my dreams.

The darkness may take a toll on the shield,
But the shield can't be destroyed,
Because I won't let it, I will protect my field;
No time to cut corners I can't avoid.

I write this out of anger, confusion,
Maybe even a little bit of fear,
Along with a lot of "why?"

God, I know my freedom;
I know my light is coming, but I just hope and pray
It comes when it is meant to come.
Until then, I protect my field,
And I look darkness in its face,
And fight for my destiny.

Jon Graham

Insecurities

Feeling like I've been played for a fool,
Not once, not even twice, but many.
I'm a victim of the uncool,
And a victim of thinking I'm in love a million times too many.

Now I fear I will be forever haunted;
I'm sick of being around where I'm not wanted.
I tried believing before, thinking it's all good,
Then something comes up, and it kills my mood.

Yes, I have insecurities, can you blame me?
Yet, many of us do, is that how it should be?
Unfortunately, I don't have an answer,
But before I conclude, I'll look in the mirror.

The man in the mirror said this:
Protect yourself, protect your heart,
Protect your soul with all your might;
You're all you've got at the end of the night.

I then walked away, but looked back.
The man in the mirror had one more thing to say back,
"Understand what I'm sayin', please know this,
You have to trust her until otherwise,
You'll need to believe in her on this."

A man's insecurities come from a past of heartbreak,
Jealousy, betrayal, envy, and self-doubt.
To be honest with myself,
I think I've become the jealous type.

A man should not get jealous with his woman;
Don't get consumed in the hype.

Women believe that we men are cold,
Destructive people with no regard for a woman's heart;
I'm a witness that women are just as cold,
And they feel nothing in time after ripping apart a man's heart.

Are my insecurities trying to protect me?
For I can't bear another blow like that to me.
Once again, it's become not me, but we,
And my insecurities have already made her leave tears on my white tee.
I have even abandoned my rule, no tears;
My insecurities are a replay of my distant, yet greatest fears.
But they've already cost me once already,
But here, right now, I don't know; give me a sign already.

The lightning strikes; the thunder roars,
Thoughts making my heart pound as the rain pours.
I cried after getting played that day;
The next day, I promised, never again will I wrongfully pay.

All I know is, if my insecurities were right,
It would take years to recover from what I've held so tight;
It would spell the end of my trust, for anyone,
And then I will most likely punish another someone.

Critical Point in Time

Losing my mind over so many things,
And they all matter because I care about all things.
Sometimes I wish my heart was as cold as this world;
Maybe then I wouldn't have thoughts that hurt my heart.

I pray that my insecurities don't destroy my future,
I keep looking in the rear-view mirror,
I love you; I want to keep telling you,
But what I can't tell you is the fear that I have.

You're a special thing in this world to me,
But I moved away from, it so I could save me;
It wasn't your fault, but I had to do it,
I was becoming unknown to myself, how the hell did it happen?

Now I'm sitting here, thinking too much,
Thinking no one is special; everybody is the same and such.
I guess it's my fault; I couldn't tell you for sure,
But the last thing I want to feel is that I was right to be insecure.

I needed to hear your voice before I went to sleep,
Because there's some nights I can't sleep because I'm thinking of you,
I don't trust people, but I trust you,
Probably the first and only one who would ride or die for me.

These days, a ride-or-die is becoming non-existent,
Too many lies and not enough energy and time spent.
I doubted you twice, and I was wrong both times;
I don't know why you stayed, but I'm blessed that you did.

I act tough, but honestly, at times I felt weak without you.
I need you in my life and hear that you need me in yours;
There was a time where I thought about life without you.
I felt it, I don't want to feel it again.

If my life was together, I'd give you this ring;
I just hope that I'm walking into forever love this time.
I'm optimistic, but hey, only God knows it all;
As I rise to the top, you were with me during my fall.

Now I'm close to rising again;
If the times were hard still, would the woman stay?
I think this one will; she's worth the chance.
When we're together, it's like no one's watching while we dance.

Jon Graham

Untitled

What am I thinking about?
Maybe about the year that was?
2013 was a year with the thought of doubt.
A year full of questions.

I helplessly and hopelessly watched the
Person I am lose touch with himself,
Losing the strength I possess,
And the very thing that described myself.

I was turning into a ghost;
Answers would not come when I needed them the most.
I turned to God with all of my pain,
Because I knew that only He knew what my future will contain.

Darkness fell and covered my world,
My sky fell before me, my last remaining light, one girl.
But as strong as that last light was,
I hated putting this on her, but that's what love does.

A love as strong as what I think this love is,
It's almost unmatched.
Beautiful, irresistible, unbreakable, secure,
Warm, safe, and magical.

I've made selfish decisions: some were a must,
And others are unexplainable, inexcusable, and led to no trust.
As I move forward, I pray that I shed my past,
And that the greatest girl I've ever had and me continue to believe in us.

The world is just full of madness;
I fell prey to it a few times, and it left me with sadness.
Yet I still wanna say, "I love you," to the world,
I would've never changed for the better, or met that one girl.

God, I want to thank You always for the people in my life;
I'm trying to do better, and be a stronger person,
Thankful for my blessings, though I'm searchin',
Looking for the promise land, wherever that may be.

Some call it, pursuit of happiness;
I call it one big game that I must win,
I want to be a champion.

And I want to share this life, this love,
The triumph, and the peacefulness with that one girl.
Her name is…

Jon Graham

2014

Why Do We Fall?

As a child, I pictured life in my own way;
Through my eyes, I saw peace, everything my way.
My first reality check brought me to Earth;
It hit me early, and kept me at bay,
But even after, I still never lost my way.

I know the devil, or whatever evil exists, is a lie,
But I hear it whisper; I look up at God in the sky.
My mind becomes clear, thanks to the peace God brings me from up so high;
I was an ambitious child waiting for my piece of the pie.

I come so far from the bottom,
Never saw the top.
I rose to become a champion, and now,
I always will be, and I will never stop.

A man's darkest time shows his true form,
Even if what seems very far from the norm.
I am a man who fell into a storm,
Almost held captive, shaken by its form.

Most of the peace and happiness I've witnessed
Was now becoming distant, missing, lost.
I've endured much pain, and much sorrow,
And there were times of thought, thinking,
At what cost?

I struggle to find peace again, drained of energy,
But I need no one's sympathy,
And I accept no one's pity.
Those are makings of a coward, in a shameful part of a city.

I've been called a hero, a symbol of hope;
If so, why does the hero fall into the dark?
How easy it seems sometimes to just give up and mope.
One of the greatest symbols of hope was that of Noah's Arc.

Why do we fall? Isn't the evil supposed to fall?
The evil does the wrong,
And the hero works and drives for righteousness.

Maybe the hero, the champion, has been given a true test;
A test of will, faith, strength, one to show his best.

Love brings me strength; it keeps me alive.
The dream drives me, to win, I strive.
The journey will always take care of itself,
Wherever it may lead, it will show it wealth.

Pretend

Been in love with the game since forever,
To fall down and not get back up, never.
Life can be as strange as the weather,
But what you love most feels as soft as a feather.

A lot of you don't know me, the real me;
Let's pretend I stopped playing basketball, still love me?
Let me pretend that nothing can ever stress me,
Or better yet, let's pretend stress is something no one can feel, can you see?

Visualize the moment, create the dream,
Feel the moment, and you reach the dream.
Easy for some, yes, it may seem,
But there's nothing like winning and reaching the goal with your team.

Can't pretend about how much I love the game;
Crazy thing is, I never worried about the fame.
I see so many who can't deal, so they then bring shame,
But my mind, my heart, my soul, they're not ones to tame.

If these are tamed, they can't grow;
When they can't grow, they fall, fall far below.
The light dims, into darkness they go,
Can we pretend I'm invincible? Can we make that so?

We don't even have to, because we are our own light,
Everyone has their own battle to fight.
This world has a lot of wrong, but let's be steady
And continue to do it right.
My dream, my triumph, is in plain sight.

Mystery it may be; question marks, they may exist.
The walk of faith may feel like a walk amongst flames;
Fear, anxiety at every corner.

But let's pretend all of that is absolutely nothing,
Because to pretend, is to visualize.
To visualize, is to live,
And to live, is to rise,
Rise to victory.

Jon Graham

2015

Revival

One season, chapter, and milestone ended,
Now a new season has begun, I'm already in it.
But this time, I'm looking for a new me;
I've got to return to the beast that I used to be.

They young and positive man I used to be,
I know he isn't gone, because he's still a part of me.
I need to revive and resurrect him for all to see,
Especially me; I'm a champion according to the prophecy.

The world may think I've lost and won't make it far,
But I'm here to tell you, you're wrong, and I'm going to show how wrong you are.
The chains are cut loose; the reigns came to a truce.
Now I'm rebuilding my empire, the Dark Knight again, no longer Bruce.

Broken heart because I couldn't save you from yourself,
Hate that I cursed your name, but I'm pissed at you and kind of at myself.
Funny thing is, I still believe in you;
Sooner or later, I'll know which you is the real you.

In the meantime, I'll be getting back to winning;
I'm keeping the wisdom of me today while going back to the beginning.
The old me is now the center of my thinking,
And if and when my dream woman comes back, I'll return the favor and do the heartbreaking.

The current me will get out of the old me's way,
That's when I'll start winning again, give myself the final say.
I'll be the beast once again; it's in there, I can sense it.
Dear God, help me revive it; I can win with it.

Jon Graham

You didn't bring me through all of this for nothing;
It's time now, everything or nothing.
I know I'm destined for greatness to be; I'm looking up, not around me.
Revival of the old me, the champion has returned.

You Know You're in Love When...

You know you're in love when you wake up wishing she was there;
You know you're in love when you can enjoy yourself with her anywhere;
You know you're in love when you're scared she'll make a fool out of you;
You know you're in love when you continue to wish things were how they were.

You know you're in love when you feel like you're losing your mind,
Losing your mind because you want her by your side.
You know you're in love when no other woman compares.

You know you're in love when you try your best to prepare,
Prepare for heartbreak, because you can't dismiss the possibility,
But to give your heart is to also be vulnerable.

If you feel any of these, you might be in love;
It's strange, but I hear it's beautiful.
I heard it's wonderful, but unpredictable,
Sometimes indescribable.

I wonder if that's how it's supposed to be,
We'll see how being in love for the first real time treats me.

Jon Graham

Untitled

Unpredictable, unforgettable, good, bad,
Or a mixture of them both, judge me how you will.

I'll just say I'm a different breed,
Like your favorite book, yet it's hard for me to read.
Life tried to run me over dead like a stampede,
Crawling my way to what I need.

I watched my college years breeze by like the winds of a hurricane,
Went from feeling superstar-ish back to feeling just plain,
Momentarily, until I woke up and stopped acting insane.

All this time, I thought I wasn't good enough,
Wasn't sure enough, wasn't cool enough,
Absent of the "it-factor."
I questioned myself, forever had doubts,
Just getting lost following multiple routes.

I guess one day, they'll look at me like I see myself in the soon-enough future;
Better than good enough,
They'll look at me and tell the other to step their game up.

No longer overlooked, or looked pass,
And I won't worry or care who's lurking to try and hurt me;
No more sitting down waiting for B.S. to pass,
I got some class.

I'm 23, thinking about things that bothered me through all of my teen years;
I didn't have the guts to step up and whisper to desire's ears.
Shot myself down before I even created my chance, then came the internal tears.

You wouldn't see me crying, but inside it was hard;
Let some good women go by, and I sat wondering,
What if I...just said hey,
Tell them who I am, and accept that this is me, and nothing is going to change.
Why would I want it to change?

But I was still afraid to be alone;
Freshman year of high school, I was already looking for a prom date of my own,
That says a lot; 15 years old thinking alone I would always roam.

Why do I still feel that kid in my psyche?
I guess new mess brings back old mess,
Especially about women and maybe jealousy;
Might be feeling that more these days lowkey.
Maybe because of trust issues, such foolery.

Jon Graham

Untitled

I wish that you could share your pain with me;
Maybe you wouldn't sound so conflicted with me.
I said from day one we'd be a team, we,
I said we'd go the distance, and that the distance wouldn't break us,
Seemed like we had the faith that we were meant to be.

Or maybe I loved us so much, I had enough love for the both of us.
I was so conflicted but continuing with team US;
I know I had B.S. with you, you didn't make me blue,
Because I love you.

Don't tell me it's over now;
We came so far, why crumble now?
Could've left more times than one,
But you stayed and saved my heart from burning in the sun.

Don't put me in that position, I'm trying to trust you,
Even though I feel this "I don't give a f***" vibe from you.
If you don't, just tell me; that's when I'll walk away from you,
And I won't come back. I'm sorry times two.

I gave you my all, because you deserved it;
I allowed my trust issues a backseat, reserved it.
Time's stopping; now my thoughts are racing faster than time,
Smile has stopped on a dime, it's my conscience inside allowing me to speak in rhyme.

Please don't tell me we have to part;
I even wrote you a song, and you know it was from the heart,
Used to sing, I can't rap, but for you I'd make up some art.

Never was intimidated; in fact, part what I love is that you're so smart

Don't change now.

Untitled

Some look into their hearts for what's real;
I visualize past the layers of my soul as I peel.
I'm fighting for what I know I can achieve;
I can feel how close I am,
My soul has importance for me to receive.

I feel alone at times of self-thought;
I guess part of it is my own doing.
Those who know me well know I play by the rules,
But more because I'm afraid to get caught.

But I no longer feel the same,
From head to toe; I want to play a different game,
Because I feel the one I've been playing is outdated.
It no longer fits me; other thoughts I've contemplated.

I can feel nothing will ever be the same;
Parts of me will, but I feel evolution in me now, even though the message already came.
Maybe I wasn't ready to allow it,
But some things can't be denied, and I can feel it.

Untitled

Here we go again, mind and heart connected,
Love is on my mind tonight; watch out, my words and thoughts might get hectic.
I was afraid to let myself go;
I worry for me more than I for you, although,
You told me, not to ever worry.
"I'm here for you, and we were meant to be,"
Oh, most definitely, I'm here to set you free.

But myself, unpredictable, like a caged black bear,
I don't want to hurt you because I've changed from my heart's wear and tear.
I blame it on my generation of women and how messed up it is now,
And I don't want the past to haunt me,
But I can feel it creeping right now.

Love is a dangerous thought,
Dangerous action like biting from fruit that unknowingly has rot.
You look in my eyes and you see a maze,
Running through my obstacle, phase by phase,
Holy treasure in the distance, only one to amaze.

Blackbird flying through the red sky,
Decimated town, full of questions starting with "why";
Explain this to me, please,
I think I'm losing my strength. I'm falling down to my knees.

And the world wants to keep me there;
I can feel the pressure, and it's obvious from where.
Most of it is my fault, thoughts I can't begin to bear,
Like a man's Pandora box, not the strongest will to share.

Jon Graham

The feeling of deception is all around me;
I'm holding on like the last leaf on a dying tree.
I wish I could clearly see what God can see,
But if I look it would take away from the lessons and the strength He's given me.

War-ready, like a soldier,
Took a hit from a runaway boulder;
Fate of the world isn't on my shoulder,
But my life is, and before it's beautiful,
Things only will get colder.

Love keeps me warm, able to keep it moving,
But day by day, it has been proven.
Feeling like I let the ones who love me most down;
Even though they didn't have to, they stuck around.

The Girl in the Golden Dress

The holiday season last year brought him more pain instead of joy,
Pain from the one he loved most; he is left looking like a confused young boy,
Heart tossed in storage like an old toy,
He became a monster, out to destroy.

Not to kill, but play with hearts like what happened to his,
Acting like he no longer knew what love is.
He was lost, blinded, defeated, trapped in a dark abyss,
But the magic of New Year's would bring him something to witness.

New Year's Eve would bring him a woman in a golden dress.
They knew each other from close encounters,
But no secret;
This New Year's Eve, they were out to impress.

The girl in the golden dress had eyes that lit up the dark room with few bits of light;
His glasses were dark, but there was no denying the girl in the golden dress was in his
sight.
Broken-hearted, acting like he was alright,
His emotions, his feelings in the moment, he continued to resist and fight.

The smile of the girl in the golden dress drew him closer,
And her lips, mmm…so soft and luscious. As she kissed him,
The fire between them would bolster.

He knew he couldn't give her what she truly wanted, and she also knew.
It wasn't her fault; this thing between them meant nothing…
Or at least is it used to.

He wanted nothing, but she wanted more;

Jon Graham

Had to admit, New Year's Eve never felt like this before.

Misunderstandings caused friction;
The girl in the golden dress was hurt, and she no longer wanted to be near his section.
To him, loving someone else was nothing more than fiction,
But this time he had to make a decision.

Still numbed from pain, he took her to his room;
She showed tears of anger and confusion,
Couldn't sweep it away with a broom.

Instead of just kissing her,
He looked into her eyes and told her how beautiful she was;
It was no longer the alcohol that created a buzz.

The girl in the golden dress smiled at him;
It was a smile that he could never forget,
No matter how much he felt grim.

It was all he could have ever hoped for (if he did) in the midst of emotional numbness,
But after it was over, he would feel backlash of his ways of the heartless.

She was gone, and he pushed it all away,
Because he went back to what he thought would be okay.
Now his heart is confused and numb today;
Some things can't be fixed, no matter what he would say.

Here we go again, New Year's is approaching,
Only this time he will be flying,
Out of state in new surroundings,
Trying to change his life and keep it moving.

If he could see her, he'd want to say how sorry he was,

How wrong he was,

How heartless he was.

His reason for that New Year's Eve not bringing stress

Was all because of the girl that was in the golden dress.

Jon Graham

2016

I Thought...

I thought it was love;
I thought it would last forever.
I thought my doubts going in were wrong;
I thought I could love you forever.

I thought I told myself I wouldn't go through this again;
I thought you said you'd love me until the universe said when.
I thought you said distance wouldn't break us apart;
I thought it was right to give this a chance, was it smart?

I thought you said you couldn't see a future without me, did you see it now?
I thought I'd get it together and get down on one knee for you; guess we'll never know now.
I thought I could start singing love songs again and stop feeling so bitter;
I thought I wouldn't feel alone in the coldest winter.

I thought I could prepare for this,
I thought someone would break my fall,
I thought I could risk it all,
I thought I could ignore the writings on the wall.

I thought I could stand heartache;
I thought that because I loved you.

I thought wrong.

Beautiful, Dangerous Love

Love is such a beautiful feeling,
And love is such a dangerous way of thinking.
Good vs. evil, courage vs. fears,
Hero vs. villain, and happiness vs. the saddest of tears.

Love is two-faced and will easily show both its sides;
Other times, the beauty of it takes over,
Yet within, the danger still resides.

The one you're in love with becomes the air you're breathing;
When they're not around, you're suffocating.
The danger is, what if she's gone and isn't coming back this time?
Oh, but the beauty of that last kiss,
The beauty of counting down to the second you kiss her again, the feeling of bliss.

Beautiful, Dangerous Love

To love is to be vulnerable;
The danger of love, defense is gone,
And you're left vulnerable.
The beauty of letting someone in is a feeling of oneness,
No longer alone, and you're shocked because you never thought it could feel like this.

Gaze into the eyes of the one you love;
You see the future that you've been dreaming of,
You see right now, a moment when time stops,
You see the pain of your past fade from your mind, fade from you heart.

A smaller, simpler way to describe the beauty
Of beautiful, dangerous love

Jon Graham

You become hooked on that gaze,
And the danger has the power to get you lost in a maze,
Amazing? Yes. I would love to still have that feeling these days.
Danger has created numbness, emptiness, now for many-a-days.

There's a poison, a danger about Friday and Saturday night,
But it's a fun poison and danger; a lust we can't fight.
Or maybe we just won't; we're addicted,
Like we can be addicted to love, you can't miss it.

Beauty is a Saturday afternoon, or a Sunday morning,
Waking up, feeling on her soft skin,
Realizing you're not dreaming;
She's right there, gazing back at you in the same bed you're in.

The danger of love is laying in that same bed alone,
Knowing that there will be no more Saturday afternoons or Sunday mornings.
The girl you dreamed about and woke up with has left, not planning to return.

Your most beautiful of dreams
Is now you're worst of nightmares, it seems.
Now you sit and wonder how,
For it was the danger of love, and its plots and schemes.

You're up late at night thinking,
Will love save me again, or am I doomed to suffering?
Would a new flame just mean nothing,
Or will it save me from endless falling?

Wake me up before you go,
Kiss me one more time before you go,

Gaze into my eyes once more;
I need a just a little more of your love...

Your beautiful, dangerous love.

Jon Graham

Untitled

They say better to have loved and lost than to have never loved at all right?
Maybe when I was younger and clueless, but today, I say they are half-right.

Almost nothing can hurt a man more
Than to realize the one he loves
Can no longer say the words, "I love you, too."
My heart is decimated, ripped, almost gone.

I now tread with caution;
Wanting to love has lost its oxygen.

I feel colder, hollow;
If someone new is looking for love, I don't think I'm one to follow,
At least not at this juncture,
Heart recovering from the puncture.

Whoever is the one to save me,
I thank God in advance for you and me.
Absolute blessing, wish come true,
Wondering next what I should do.

Damn, the little things I miss,
Used to feel like a vacation, escaping reality with just a kiss.
Never had too much to say much about it;
We could sense the pain behind it.

You held me, I held you;
Doors locked, dimmed lights, and you.
For a little bit of time, any negativity of the day didn't matter;

The inevitability of tomorrow, didn't matter,
Rather, just me and you and the bedcovers we gather.

Domino effect, one thing after another falling,
How much losing must a champion endure before he realizes his calling?
His face is dry, but inside he cries
Hysterically; he's balling.

I'm not talking basketball though;
What happened to how much you loved me so?
Are we supposed to forget everything that happened though?

"Life goes on"? That's the coldest thing you've ever said to me;
Never said, "I love you, too," to me,
Telling me you're living your life, I see,
Quit acting like I don't know what that means.

I want to scream f*** you,
Because of how deep in love I fell for you.
One day, I laugh because saying, "Damn, how stupid was that?"

Change of heart, it's going to take
Worthiness for me to change back,
Crawl back to love?
It'd be excessive to budge towards love.

Right now, anyway…

We spend more of our energy trying
To impress the ones who could care less about us,
And with less effort, we hurt the ones that love us.

Jon Graham

My mentality is fragile;
How you love is intangible.
No amount of relocation or other
Changes could change amoré. It's not expendable,
It's priceless, undeniable.

Hate is too much energy draining,
And I don't think you're worth it;
Foolishly try as I might, but
I'll never be perfect.

2017

Why?

Why? Why did I not see it?
Why did I screw this up?
Why didn't I realize before it was too late,
To realize that you were supposed to be mine?
In this case of ours, why didn't I cross that line?

A blessing in disguise you were,
A period of blindness wouldn't allow me to concur.
Now all I can do is think, about where we were,
Think about how someone else is enjoying
What could've, and maybe, what should've been
Part of my future,
And how I just remember the mistake I made at an important juncture.

Why?

Why am I falling in love with you?
Why do I want so bad for you to let me love you?
Why does it feel like I'd have to give up so much for us to ever be possible?
Why do I ever care enough to allow this to feel important?

We all should be cautious,
Because love is unpredictable, and even dangerous,
The thought of it makes me nauseous.

Why, in spite of it all, do I feel like you're worth it?
Why, in my eyes, do I think you're perfect?
Why in my heart do I feel like you deserve it?
I must be drunk.
Why?

Why can't I get you out of my head,
Out of my dreams, and out of my nightmares?
I don't want you in my dreams because you're haunting me,
And I don't want you in my nightmares because of the beautiful time you gave me.

It's clear that you've let me go,
So why can't I do the same?
Why do I feel like I met you at the wrong time?
Why couldn't you be strong for me this time?

At a time when now I really needed you, you cut ties, why?
Why couldn't I be better than I was?
I guess now, we'll never really know why.

Jon Graham

The Fake Love Effect

As I look through my timelines,
While the cold weather vanishes, I can feel the signs,
Starting to see more of the hugged-up and, yes, the cuffed-up,
What's the change? Aging? Or is it just fake love that's rising up?

Seasonal love? Oh, because when it's cold,
We all need a little something to warm up with,
And I'm not talking about a blanket; we're more bold,
But it seems like when it gets warm
Something changes for most, so I've been told.

Layers are coming off, and I don't just mean clothes;
Sun is out, here comes that breeze,
And the beach? Done deal; for a man,
Seeing girls in bikinis, his mind is like
"I gotta have her," and he gets her with ease.

But wait, wasn't that the same girl on Instagram a few months back?
When she was cold and cooped up in the sack
With some guy? And the caption said, "This is a forever thing."
Here she is, flaunting the goods in your face;
She knows what she's doing, and he knows he doesn't see a ring

As a man, do I dare bite the bait?
Sexual tension is burning, damn…
You can feel it in the air as she's looking at you like,
"Yo, please don't make me wait."

Apparently, she's single…for the moment.
Does her man know that? You sure? Take a moment.

Moment's passed; now back to walking out of this club to a quieter setting,
Can't ignore that one irresistible, burning, raw, natural component.

I think you know what's next

Spring break is over; that wild weekend is over,
And for some, that little "off period" is over,
That "hall pass" is used up,
Let's get back to being complicated after the turn-up.

A few days later, you see back on your timeline,
"I love you, missed you so much, bae,"
#hubby #soulmate
Inside, I laugh hysterically,
I feel almost compelled to comment with a crying laughing emoji.
How about #bullshit

In my eyes, I don't care;
Don't know the guy, and she obviously didn't care.
No, not that night; it's almost unfair,
Not fair how she threw it back and talking big game while doing it,
Sheesh, that's that shit right there.

But hey, I'm not going to ruin a "happy" home,
Just wouldn't be surprised before curving season ends
That when I call, she just might pick up the phone.

But let me get serious.

I think there are some lingering effects,
Long-term possibly, attention of the mind, body, heart, and soul it directs;
A man meets an absolutely beautiful woman who he can see a future just as bright as her
Contagious smile, he'd take bets.

Jon Graham

But it remains unclear if she likes him the way he likes her;
He used all his tricks and tactics,
But he still can't for sure read her.
The last thing he needs is another train-wreck,
Or another "surprise," and then he thinks for a second...

She's not the girl from the timeline;
She's not designated for the hotline.
He feels like he's getting burned for putting himself out there,
He thinks he's going to have this woman, but at the same time, he thinks she's thinking,
"Have me where?"

Love is such a twisted emotion,
And it involves the most complex, complicated people:
Women.

He thinks he loves this woman;
At the same time, he heeds the warnings given to him by the women from his timeline.

But who wants to stay alone?
Who wants to sit back and watch someone they have strong feelings for
Walk into the arms another man (woman)?
And how many good women are left?

Does he even deserve a good woman after his actions?

And will he have to risk it all
To just hope and pray she'll break his fall?

Rage Release

How would you feel if you won't get to love the love of your life anymore?
If you couldn't see her anymore?
Knowing that she's happier with you not there anymore?
You're feeling what I'm feeling... RAGE.

So much sadness and hurt, which eventually morphs and merges into such anger,
A type of anger with blinding potential,
Which for some could spell a form of danger.
I fight my rage every single day since things changed,
Since she became a stranger,
An enemy; the deepest love is now a dark memory I despise,
Level of hate, major.

But it's not just her; it's the one thing I thought would change my life forever.
Truth be told, despite it being a failure, it's still changed my life forever.
I just don't know if it was for the better,
Left with rage when I dreamed of being a trend-setter.

Blind fury, anger, sadness, confusion, little irritation eats away.
That's how I define the rage I'm feeling every day,
Praying that God will show me a different way,
Because this is hard to deal with and hard to act like it's nothing to talk about or say.

Truth be told, basketball has been a source of my rage, building the last five plus years,
And yet, ironically, it's what I do to release my rage because it's hard for me to shed tears;
Nothing worse than seeing the worst of your fears.
I know how dark this sounds, but I have to let my rage out somehow,
Sorry if it hurts your ears.

I almost wish I quit ball years ago just to be with you;
I may have regretted it, but I wonder if I'd be happier with you.

Jon Graham

Now I may never feel that love again,
And it's my fault that I feel like I hate you,
Only because I loved you that much;
I wish I never met you.

Just not at the time that I did.
I was a kid with much immaturity;
At the same time, I didn't understand the art of purity.
I turned into the most devilish form of me that anyone will ever see,
And when I left, I watched the greatest love I ever had die right in front of me slowly.

And the reason I left you behind is taking its time to kill me inside; it's trying,
I'm fighting it off, but it's no secret I've been losing.
Some days, it's hard to get up and fight again because of the un-knowing,
Or is it waiting on the inevitable, on everything I'm wondering.

The one who I need doesn't seem like she wants to save me;
Sounds pathetic, but I wish I could tell her I love and I wanna be
The best version of me for her,
Ask her what kind of future she can see,
And is it really with me or not, can you set me free?

Being around you numbs my rage to the point of little existence,
But because you aren't mine, that feeling is only like temporary resistance.
I wish things worked out like I planned when I was a kid, but don't we all?
I just think my family and I would be happier as well.

And I wouldn't feel all this rage,
With this rant of a rhyme I release part of my rage;
It may haunt me for a long time, but to God, I'm thankful that I can portion-by-portion
release my rage.

Revolving, Walking Time Bomb

Revolving means recurring, to repeat
Itself again, and again, and again. Same action.
When we think about time bombs,
We think of explosions, and destruction.

Bombs destroy whatever is in the vicinity,
Leaving nothing behind but a memory.

Now merge the word revolving with time bomb;
Now merge yourself in there.
Now you've created the ultimate qualm.

Imagine having something so beautiful,
And you have it caressed in your arms.
You have a chance to free yourself
Of the pain that this "toxin" has caused,
To you it only harms.

Beautiful eyes, soft skin,
Luscious lips, it's all in front of you in your hands,
But then somehow you prevent yourself
From meeting seemingly easy demands.

Sometime later... *BOOM!*
You've destroyed a golden opportunity at happiness
With a beautiful woman inside and out.
She's gone, and you're back to loneliness;
All you can hold onto now is the aftermath
Of the destruction you've caused throughout.

You haven't lost it all.
You've been blessed with another chance after all;
Someone else wants to save you and break your fall.
You look at her, and she gazes back at you,
Grabbing you to come closer, her back's against the wall.

You feel love for her,
She even admitted to you that she wanted to be with you,
The revolving, walking time bomb that you've become.

Why?

Maybe she has love for you back,
But you wouldn't let the toxin out of you,
And now the time bomb is refueled,
And it's once again ready to attack.

BOOM! BOOM!

You've found a way to destroy another
Beautiful, rejuvenating possibility.
She's gone; she's not coming back.
Why would she come back?

Look around, you're all messed up now;
Look around, that warm feeling you had
Has disappeared, decimated, and how?

How is the ultimate question.

...Maybe I've become a revolving, walking time bomb,
And I'm the triggerman.

For Her

How amazing and beautiful you are,
And how unfortunate I can only now admire from afar.
But it was because of my doing
That you and I may never be;
Capacity for forgiveness is different in each of us,
So I cannot blame you for holding it against me.

For her, my only regret
Was not telling you how messed up the situation was;
Maybe I should've given you a chance,
And you'd find it in your heart to understand what it was.

And I regret not choosing you,
But in that moment in time, I didn't know where to turn to.
I didn't even come at you aggressively;
You were the aggressor, but I worried about
The consequences I'm dealing with right now.
You met me at my worst, mad excessive,
Because you deserve the best, an example of progressive.

I'll just keep in my distant dreams,
I may have killed my only chance it seems;
Sometimes my mind may not be at ease under that duress
Until the next time I hold you in my arms
And gaze into your eyes, this one's for her.

Jon Graham

Girls Like You

Those girls like you remind me why I second-guess relationships;
It's funny because it's ones like you who actually are in full-on relationships,
Posting pics with a caption saying,
"Wish you knew how I much I loved you,"
And I'm like, "Hahaha, yeah. I wish this man had some kind of clue…"

Wouldn't get far with girls like you,
Part of the reason my heart's turned blue;
You say you're just heartbroken, yeah? Me too.
You say you play a lot of games; guess I do too.

Damn, the girls like you send a lot of men over the edge,
So much a man would go so far as to have you;
Sad of me to say, but it's reality—watch the news. This violence
There's no shortage.

Girls like you wield a lot of power.
Send one man home; meet another within the hour.
Devious and dangerous, but shine like the sunflower,
Good men have that fear, no shame for them to cower.

Then they're girls like you, little more worth it,
All the extra miles, all the money we spent,
Just to see you,
But because of the past, you want to work for it.

Can't mess up with girls like you;
Girls like you may forgive, but you'll never forget to
Hold it against us when we
Try to make a case for another chance to

Show you that it was a tough situation. Who
In the right mind can explain something like this to you
Without you storming off and losing faith in this good man with spots of bad luck?
It's true.

2018

What I Hate About Love

I hate love; at this point it feels stupid to have believed.
Emotionally, pushing towards crushes just gets me crushed,
Only because of one stupid mistake from a chapter of the past I've regretted;
From its effects, I've regressed.

I hate what love does to me;
It turns me into a daydreamer about what can be,
Then reality reminds me that it's just not going to happen,
then mentally I fall to the ground like
I fell out of a tree.
It was perfect; I would've seen my image of perfect—her—is what I would see.

Not through a snap or IG story, not through a picture,
But in my arms, my hands running through her hair, instead of admiring a filter.
No secret, if she was here, I'd be much happier,
Instead of walking around looking stupid and at times, totally off-kilter.

I hate love for turning me into this,
Feeling like I'm holding a boulder over my head to stay alive.
I just wanted to thrive…

I hate love for making me think that she would love me the way I think I do for her;
I use the words "I think" because I'm not even truly sure about me and her.
Maybe my idea of what love is isn't exactly true…
I mean, the ocean isn't exactly what I first pictured as blue.

I hate that love made me delusional,
Thinking that I was going to have a storybook ride
to married life with the first girl I ever loved.
I felt like we were unstoppable;

Feels like a joke now, and the joke ended up being on me.
For a while, the heartbreak was unbearable,

Then I wised up and realized what a fool I was,
Should've known better (this is the part where you pretend it's now laughable).

I hate love for making me think she ever really cared for me to begin with—
Again. How foolish of me, when will I learn?
Love is a dangerous thing to yearn;
I'm left standing, watching and enduring my heart burn to the ground into ashes,
And it'd be ridiculous of me to think she'd have any concern.

I hate love because I gave all of my heart to the wrong one,
And now there's almost nothing left for the right one.
I don't know why I'm still talking about this, because it shouldn't matter anymore.
Now that I think, it's not even just that day in the past,
It's the destruction; it's left me in its wake,
And what it turned me into, I wasn't me anymore.

I became the instrument of my own demise,
Knowing what I was doing, so no wonder it's not a surprise.
No surprise why I'm standing in the epicenter of the freshly made ruins,
Where the fallen will not rise.

It's no surprise why sometimes I hate love.

Jon Graham

Untitled

Way too many nights with no sleep,
Lost opportunities feel like cuts that run deep;
Hate that I made a promise I was never sure I could keep.
Hurtful times wanting tears, so I can let go,
This is a hurdle that is hard to leap.

You deserve the moon and the stars,
But understand loving me means dealing with my scars;
Loving me is complicated, like choosing between the best cars,
Wishful thinking, talking to the moon like I'm Bruno Mars.

Not just an "I want you," but more like "I crave you,"
Different level of desire, if you only knew;
I'd be smiling a little more again if you felt it, too.
Maybe that's a dream that ain't meant to come true.

Climbing a mountain of challenges;
Guess I'll meet you at the top if it balances,
Ready to let go of what made me more cold and more heartless,
Because how I can learn that level of love again
With that type of ignorance?

You weaken me every single time I give a care,
So when you did leave, almost couldn't say it wasn't fair;
Never loved and now hated anyone more than you.
Can't get you out of my hair,
Our past now feels like nothing but wear and tear.

To Be Continued...

Throughout it all, it's only been you,
Through the grind, through the heartbreak,
And the rage, it's been impossible to have a day go by
Without thinking about you.

I'm not sure how much longer I can go without releasing my confessions;
Not sure how much longer I have to act
Like I'm not in love with you,
Still regretting my past actions.

All I want to do is tell you how much I want to love you,
How much I want to be your everything, or whatever I can be for you;
Your king, and only yours.
Although you'd be any man's dream come true,
the feeling you give me feels like paradise;
I just wish you could feel it too.

From your beautiful eyes, to your wonderful smile,
From the moment I walked through that door and saw you,
I found myself dazed for a long while.

I just want to know how I can make this right,
Because being without you just doesn't feel right;
Daydreaming half of the day, into my dreams at night,
My heart is addicted to you, it craves you,
My shining light at the end of the tunnel,
A queen who is worth the fight.

Among me walks a Goddess;
Losing you forever would be one of my greatest losses.

Jon Graham

Loving you is teaching me how to love again;
Even if it's dangerous, I'm becoming willing to take a chance again.

The Truth Within My Walls

Doomed? Or am I just lost?
Lost in my own twisted fantasy, my mind
Messed up, crisscrossed;
Feeling like my heart's been tossed.
Guess my love wasn't worth the cost.

Hopeless romantic, lately emphasized on the word hopeless,
know I'm better, but she'd rather be senseless
And choose that other guy over me like it's effortless.
Love you better than he ever could have,
not even a contest, but you'd rather have less.

Do I have love all wrong,
Believing in that stupid love song?
I mean to say songs. Damn, I haven't felt that kind of love in so long.
Wasn't even enough to write you a love song.

I'm trapped in a space with women trying to "figure themselves out,"
And some are a long distance away from me,
So there's no point in even trying to figure it out;
All I have is little old me and all that I'm about,
But it's clear that it's not enough for women I love
But what is the point in being upset?
I had my chance to erase all doubt.

I'm the instrument of my own destruction,
Held myself back from being happy by
Masking behind seduction;
No deeper feeling with it because I was lost
And used women time and time again like an addiction,
And now the fact of the matter is my pain is not fiction.

Jon Graham

I love you better than you love yourself, and I don't like it,
Because maybe if you loved yourself more, me and you would be together,
And I swear we'd be it.
I hate that I'm just imagining and picturing;
I can't stand for this anymore; I need to sit.
If only I didn't blow it when I had the chance
Or my timing changed just a little bit.

That's the thing that drives me CRAZY,
Because she is the one that makes my mind all hazy,
She never ceases to amaze me;
Damn, right now, she should be my lady,
Making me the happiest man this side of the Mississippi.

But instead, I'm up all night writing.
Emotions screwed up; I'm jaded; they call it drake-ing…
Left on read and blown off,
When asking a distraction out to dinner, truth is,
I just don't want to be alone while I'm eating.
Some distractions had potential, but damn, even that's not working.

I guess God wanted me to ask myself why:
Why use my time and money on women
With just pretty faces and crazy curves,
But instead I got curved, no reply.
All of this got me thinking love is a lie;
At least, for me, I'm wondering why,
Because I used to be so superfly.

Tried to be a dawg, but that didn't work,
Because I have emotions, and that's enough to irk,
Irk the hell out of me, make me go berserk.

She was wild, I'm lost in the madness;
This is more fun than tripping off romance.

But it only lasted just one night,
She might go home, but she isn't about to hold me tight,
And tell me it's going to be alright.
Man, I really lost this fight.

I need my shining light
In this dark abyss called "my struggle,"
But I just want her to shine bright,
And she knows I want to love her with all of my might;
The way she makes me feel is out of sight.

Hurting me, knocking me down on one knee,
Starting to lose faith in true love quickly;
That kind of magic doesn't happen frequently,

Pray for me,
I won't ask you to take my pain from me.

Just love me,
Like I've loved you for so long.

But damn me,
Because of me, you and I may never be.

Let's Be Honest

Let's be honest; I've been lost for quite a while.
Denial only hurts me; I don't know how much longer I can keep my smile.
I don't know if I can walk another mile,
Stuck in the prison of my not so fond
Memories; suppression opened that file.

Let's be honest, still love you after all this time
And what you turned me into;
That's why I hate you, but it's still occupying
Space in my heart, and damn, I don't need you to.

I want to free myself before I let this darkness consume me,
But that's tough; back then with you and me,
Forever was all I could see.

Let's be honest.

Honestly, I know you don't care anymore,
So why should I give a fraction of my energy anymore?
Loving me is complicated, but love, period, has left me
Scarred up and sore,
Not just one, but it's multiple girls
Showing me how crappy the world can be like I've gone on tour.

Let's be honest, I wish I never met you;
At least, not when I did meet you.
I was just a kid in way over his head,
Thinking that I could save you from yourself;
In the end you left my heart for dead.

Cold and cracking, like thin ice,
I'll be damned if I go through this twice;
Maybe it's because I was too nice,
But that's me; it's always been me,
Seems like it will always be me.
You aren't worth a change from that.

I will no longer allow myself to be a prisoner

I let you put me there

Let's be honest.

Jon Graham

Freedom of The Heart

My beautiful soul, I must be honest to you,
As well as myself; I will not hold hate any longer with you.
I was wrong to do so for so long; I've tried to hide what is true.
I got angry because I lost what is owned by very few.

You were my best friend, my salvation, my peace;
It was never perfect, but then again, there was no equal.
It was a really long movie that needed no sequel;
Nothing was better on this side of the east.

I became bitter of how we ended;
I realize now, instead I should be thankful
Of how we began and how we ascended.
Out of anger and hatred within, I called our time a waste.
Now I understand that the time we had was
Something that most may wish they had or may never have had a taste.

I only hurt now because I loved you
More than life itself, more than what I deemed
The center the of my universe, and for a long time I knew.

I pretended, I acted, tried to make myself
Believe that I hated someone,
Someone who reached my soul,
Someone who taught me what head-over-heels love is like;
That someone.

I hope now that you're happy,
Happier than you ever were with me;
My only regret is that I couldn't give you all

That you wanted from me,
And those daydreams we had may not ever be.

But I thank you, for being the first true love I've ever known,
For memories and adventures, and the loyalty you'd shown.
I was not perfect, and I made bad mistakes, yet
You still loved, gave me strength in person and by phone,
And you came and made me laugh and smile when I felt alone.

Part of me fell off the map,
A dark cloud fell on my lap,
I let it take over me, into its control I began to tap,
But no more; I release my heart from hatred's trap.

Jon Graham

My New Dream

I've let go of the dark cloud that I allowed to stay;
Now that I'm free, I have a new dream; I want to follow a new pathway.
We've heard this story before likely, but if I may,
For my new dream, I've got something to say.

It's her who is my new dream,
Loving her more than I ever loved and craved that sweet French vanilla ice cream.
Cupid didn't hit me with an arrow when we met;
It felt like he shot me with a laser beam.
Hesitant because we all know all that glitters
Is not gold,
And all isn't always what it may seem.

But my new dream, her, I feel like you're everything
I could ever wish for;
Beautiful eyes I love the most, the thought of us
Is something I truly crave for.
Working out every day, thinking about you, may make my body sore,
But it's better than sitting in my room
Letting this love, this craving, my new dream rock me to my core.

But newsflash, it already has;
Walking among me is a goddess, pretty girl
With just the right amount of sass.
Rare combination of drop-dead gorgeous
And knock-your-socks-off intelligence,
She's my new dream, my curly-haired princess.

I know our time isn't right now, and maybe I'm just not that one;
If so, I've got to ease up and be steady,

But I promise if and when God says our time is now,
I'll be ready.

She's my new dream, been a dream for a while now;
B-day just passed, happy belated, bet she's partying now.
Every time I see her pretty face, I mean, just wow.

Every time she walks by, I bet the room slows down;
I bet, because my heart was beating fast back when me and her sat down,
Just to check in. For me, it didn't matter what part of town;
I'm here for my new dream. Her voice is my favorite sound.

Until then, I'm doing me, but I just had to say,
I'm stuck on my new dream, and for the time being,
I don't see that just going away.

Sorry, but I'm really not sorry.

Jon Graham

2019

Dear Valentine

Dear Valentine, every time I looked at you, I saw the closest thing to perfection,
And just in a split second came this strong connection:
To love is a desire to fulfill your partner's satisfaction,
Emotionally, physically, psychologically. But it's about more than just words; it's about action.

Dear Valentine, the thought of you was always so calming,
Like I'm on an island listening to the sound of waves crashing…
Wishful thinking, but paradise is where I wanted to take you,
Because paradise is what you brought me every time I thought of you,
And in the few times that I ever saw you.

Dear Valentine, maybe I'm just not it;
Maybe I was always missing something you desired that
Would've made me and you a good fit.
Maybe I was only meant to have one chance
To claim my chair at the table where you sit,
One chance at your heart, one chance to keep our spark lit.

Dear Valentine, I knew early on that you were going to be special,
I just had a feeling about you, and it's was way deeper than just physical.
Maybe I loved you more than you loved yourself,
And maybe more than you would've ever loved myself.

Dear Valentine, at times I wish I didn't love you as much as I do.
I thought it would fade with time like lust would usually do,
But it didn't, because it simply wasn't lust.
But to love is to do whatever it takes to make someone happy; it's a must,
Even at the expense of my own happiness.

Dear Valentine, at my worst, and during
My worst time you kept me afloat and up,

At the very moment when I felt like I'd drown
Into this drink in my cup.

You looked in my eyes with your heart in your hands;
Instead of letting myself be free, I refused to
Give into my heart's true demands.
I turned my back on you and chose misery;
I never wanted to break your heart,
But after everything that happened,
Nothing was supposed to be anything more than just some company.

Then I thought, maybe I should stop hoping that this
Crazy dream of mine would come true.
It wasn't healthy, and it felt better to tear
Myself away, but I was stuck on you like glue.

I hope you achieve all that you desire,
And that a good man reignites your passion and fire.
Maybe I'm that good man, or maybe I'll never be that lucky.

Regardless,

Happy Valentine's Day to my Dear Valentine.

Jon Graham

Silence Breaker

Fed up over the perception of men that look like me,
I want way more than what most of the world expects me to be.
I come from a city where making it to 25 is an exceptional accomplishment,
But life hasn't even started yet;
We haven't begun to own an establishment.

Every day, we wake up as targets;
We're under a microscope, fitting of what's expected of us,
very little, and why not, overall, we think less of ourselves.
We're killing ourselves instead of protecting ourselves.

Devaluing ourselves based on how light-skinned
Or how dark skinned we look,
Where's the love?
There is beauty in all of us people;
The future of my generation with
Social media honestly has me shook.

I bet the hateful and the corrupt are sitting back laughing,
Thinking "they're doing our job for us" they're sitting back chilling."
Seems like all we're doing is assisting,
But I want way more than what I've been mentioning.

Slow Down

Loving you every day is so easy because you're beautiful;
Loving me is complicated. I wish it was that simple.
Only because I strive for perfection when it comes to you,
I almost feel pathetic because I wear my heart on my sleeve;
I just wonder sometimes if you think of me too.

She deserves it because she's perfect,
Even though I'll never ask for a woman to be that,
But I just need a woman that makes it all worth it.
Number one selection and after that, there's not even a list,
Because at that point, you know that no one can compare;
Everything else fades into the mist.

I hope whoever is the one shows me that loving me is simple;
Maybe I've just made it so complex,
And it's become maze within my mind. It's all mental.

I like me better than ever; I've got the old me beat.
There's nothing like realizing your growth in faith and
Growth in love. Who knew it would feel this sweet?

Jon Graham

What If I Told You?

What if I told you that you took over my heart,
Mind, and soul morning, midday, and night?
It's you before breakfast and work,
And it's you before I sleep; it just feels right.

What if I told you I'd feel like a fool telling you all of
These feelings that I keep inside?
Felt like I'm doing us both a favor by just keeping it buried,
Lost in my rhymes is where I confide.

What if I told you I thought you were the most
Beautiful woman in the world to me?
You shine brighter than stars,
Warmed me up like the sun did today,
It's a lot, but it's just what I see.

Even if you asked me about what I see,
I don't know what I'd say, even if I was just talking to me.
I can't really explain, but I see such a light in you;
I picture great things for you,
I see you reaching your goals and becoming an even better you.

What if I told you I just think you're that special?
Again, it's hard to explain why, but I can feel it,
Revolving around my mental,
Thinking about you feels clinical;
I pray for your happiness even if feelings aren't,
Or will never be mutual.

What if I told you I'd go back in time if I could
And try to fix everything? But then again,

What if that's the worst thing I ever could do?

I'll never know; tell me who would?

What if I told you I cared more than I ever have before for someone in my life?

What if I told you I wish I didn't feel this way?

It's crazy because some days it annoys me;

Some days it makes me feel like I'm on cloud 9 like a sunset at the bay.

Life goes on; I'll deal with it if it's just a dream to me.

What if I told you I think you're the one, and I've thought that for a long time now?

Dream Talk

The more I think about the past, the more it haunts me,
But it also reminds me of what I was and gives
Me at least an idea of what I'm meant to be.
Tunnel vision, cutting off what I think isn't
Important enough to see,
A map to the goal allowing my heart and mind to be free.

Annoyed by confusion and complication,
Because I feel like it's more simple than we all think,
But instead, we just create a situation.
Maybe to a lot of us, it's more fun that way;
Simple can be basic, boring, disappointing like a limitation.

Wise words said no matter what just be yourself;
Crazy to think there was a time when I didn't
Think that I was enough without wealth,
But foolishly I did, and to be honest,
The world still makes me think about that more than being thankful for good health.

Loving myself more than ever,
Yet my walls are up higher and thicker than ever;
Part of it comes from running into the same
Old stories while finding what some may call "one's forever,"
Was chasing it part of the problem?
It's in the past, so at some point, it becomes whatever.

We can't fit the mold that makes everyone happy;
Trust me, I've tried. Foolishly I've tried,
And in the process, I stopped caring much about whether or not I'm happy.

The best version of me is right now a work in progress;
Also a long, long way from the train-wreck that was an absolute mess.
Damaged from the past, but rejuvenated,
Scarred, but healed, hungry for success.
The best version of me is way to dope to stress.

That sounds better than just good enough to me.
I hate that I wasted time questioning that, too blind to see
That we're our own prize to be.
Who cares if others don't recognize? Let yourself be free.

Jon Graham

Signed by a Hopeless Romantic

My racing mind slows down, and truth is revealed as I start sipping;
My confidence skyrockets, and I stop caring,
Then hours later my head is pounding.
But now I'm at point, I'm also thinking,
imagining, and questioning.

What's the dream of a hopeless romantic?
To one day gaze in the eyes of the love of his life?
Sounds like it would take magic.
I hear, "Just shoot your shot," but understand that for some, it's just a little problematic.
Sounds easy, sounds good, but then it sounds nerve-wracking, super hectic.

I'll be honest; the best we can do is be who we are.
I mean really be who we really are;
Change one square inch of me, and you'll have a totally different me,
If it's not clearly for the better, then it shouldn't be.

We can improve us,
But it can take time, and a hopeless romantic will think he will miss the bus.

If that bus takes off without you, then what are you really missing?
Love? Nah. Love is destiny; a story already in writing.
Destiny will always circle back around for you; that's its planning.
It will test you, and if you're as deep in love as you say you are,
Then at some point, that bus with the one for you will be stopping,
Leveled up with you.
She'll have that look for your eyes only,
And the moment will be mind-blowing.

But then there are bad situations for some hopeless romantics,
So I have to ask them,

What's a man's love to a woman's afterthought?

To me, it may be exactly what it sounds like.

But Dear Hopeless Romantic, don't change a thing;
Don't change one bit, many in this world,
Including you will sometimes confuse or
Misjudge what's real with what's nothing,
What's not that serious, what's a joke,
A waste of time, just a fling.
Guard your heart, but also let it sing;
The destined one will be listening.

Learn, get better, but don't change,
Feel that pain, don't deny it, it is what it is,
Nothing about it is strange.
Attempts will fail, you may lose and miss a good one, or two,
But a great one, a destined one, if you believe, God will arrange.

Until then, stay up.

Signed,
A hopeless romantic.

Speak from the Heart More

Speak from the heart more,
In the past what felt like forever, you were the one I used to adore;
You had my heart dancing in circles all day and all night like a world tour,
Then you made my heart melt off of my sleeve
And drop to the floor.

Speak from the heart more.

Stopped hiding, quit denial, quit playing pretend;
Well, maybe I pretended a little about me and you.
It was a story in which I was far from the end.

It was a story about a prince on the doorstep of becoming king,
He gazed into the eyes of his princess, who made his heart joyfully sing.
The prince wanted to be at his absolute peak,
At his best, and leave nothing,
For to him, his princess was perfect, and he wanted
To achieve nothing short of greatness
Before he gave his beautiful princess a ring.

Speak from the heart more.

From my first thoughts at sunrise, to my
Thoughts at night before I sleep,
You were the one I dreamt of; my stolen heart
Was yours to keep,
For you, I wasn't afraid to take the leap.

Speak from the heart more

I was in love with you,
And truth is, I was ever since I first laid eyes on you.
You were the one before I ever really knew;
You were my sky at its brightest blue.

Speak from the heart more.

If I never got the chance to show that what
I felt for you was more than just words,
I had to at least be honest with myself and let them out;
Wasn't doing this for clout,
It's not what I'm about.

My heart is on my sleeve,
Not sure that love will ever truly leave.
I felt pathetic for saying all of this because
I didn't think these were feelings that you'd ever retrieve,
But for my poems, my songs, and my letter I wrote for you long ago,
I had hoped one day you'd receive.

Speak from the heart more.

I loved you.

Letter to Self

Dear JG,

We've come such a long way since freshman year at Penn State. Priceless memories, unforgettable moments, and we've met special people along the way. As you grew and matured, your writing did as well. This hidden talent, this hidden passion and release now is a big part of you now. For a long time, you were fearful of showing your writings to anyone because you were worried about how it would make you look. Yes, you're opening a door that you've kept shut for a very long time, and that can be scary, but I am so proud of how strong and brave you are for putting this together. In this time frame (2011-2019), you've learned what true love feels like, and what true heartache felt like as well. As the great Aubrey "Drake" Graham once said, "I know they say the first love is the sweetest, but that first cut is the deepest."

With all that you've been through you've started questioning yourself, and who you are as a person. But I want you to know that your family and friends love you just the way that you are. So please, don't change who you are. Just keep being you. I hope there is a volume two of this story. If there will be one, I can't wait to see what you'll have in store for us.

Until next time